M000012186

Elizabeth Thorn

Wartime Caretaker of Evergreen Cemetery

Kathryn Porch and Susan M. Boardman

GETTYSBURG PUBLISHING

Elizabeth Thorn representing the women of Gettysburg who aided the cause in various ways". (Sue Boardman)

Published by Gettysburg Publishing, LLC

Please visit us at www.gettysburgpublishing.com

Copyright © 2013
By Susan M. Boardman and Kathryn Porch

Front Cover Images: Daguerrotype of Elizabeth Thorn
Courtesy of Brian Kennell, Evergreen Cemetery, Gettysburg,
PA

Evergreen Cemetery Gatehouse
Photograph by Matthew Brady courtesy of the Library of
Congress

Back Cover Image:
Photograph by Brian Kennell, Evergreen Cemetery,
Gettysburg, PA

Cover Design by Lisette Magaro

Printed in the United States of America
ISBN 978-0-9838631-6-8

Table of Contents

Acknowledgements

*The authors wish to acknowledge the assistance
and support of the following individuals:*

Brian Kennell
Arthur Kennell
Elle Lamboy
Cynthia Thorn Baynham
Jennie Knox, Gettysburg Photo, LLC
Lisette Magaro, Cover Design
Ben Neely, Director, Adams Co. Historical Society
Ron and Alice Tunison
Ken Boardman
Brent LaRosa

In Memoriam Ron Tunison

This volume is dedicated to the memory of sculptor Ron Tunison. He was a meticulous visual historian and a kind friend. I had the honor to witness the creation, from conception to dedication, of the Women's Memorial in Evergreen Cemetery. His contributions to the Gettysburg Battlefield stand among the great works of military monumentation.

Among Ron's historical sculptures are the portrait statue to General Samuel Wiley Crawford at the base of Little Round Top, the Masonic Friend-to-Friend Monument in the National Cemetery Annex, the Women's Memorial depicting Elizabeth Thorn in Evergreen Cemetery, and the bronze bas relief on the Delaware State Monument along Taneytown Road.

Introduction:

According to the history books, the story of the Battle of Gettysburg ended when the armies departed on July 4, 1863. But for the citizens of Gettysburg, their story was just beginning. Many survived three days (July 1-3, 1863) of battle that raged around and through their farms and homes and were left alone to pick up the pieces. To a casual observer, Elizabeth Thorn was no different than all of the other civilians doing their part to restore their town from the devastation of war. However, upon further investigation, she was very different. No other woman in town was a six-month pregnant mother, who simultaneously managed both a household and a cemetery, and acted as sole caretaker to two aging parents. No other woman was asked to dig nearly a hundred soldiers' graves. Elizabeth performed all of these strenuous tasks in the heat and the stench of a battlefield of bodies left to rot in the hot summer sun. This is her story and the story of the Evergreen Cemetery, a small-town burial ground that acquired national fame.

Section One:
Leaving Germany

Neither the Massers nor Peter Thorn left any account of what brought them to the United States in the middle of the 19th Century. But, they were not the only Germans arriving in America during that time period. In 1854, Elizabeth Masser and her parents were just 3 of the approximately 200,000 German immigrants that year alone. The reasons that propelled them to pick up their lives and move across the ocean were probably a combination of the reasons that all of the other immigrants had at that time and continue to have today: high unemployment in their home country, no opportunities, lack of land, political unrest, revolutions and war. In 1848, the German states experienced a failed revolution. They had tried, unsuccessfully, to unite into one nation. The fallout from this attempt included high unemployment and political unrest. Many Germans moved to the United States to escape these poor conditions.

The Masser family moved from Eichelsdorf, a small town outside of Frankfurt am Main in Bavaria, in southeastern Germany. Peter Thorn emigrated from Fischbach, Germany, near the western border of Frankfurt am Main, in the Taunus mountain range.

Section Two:
Moving to Gettysburg

In 1854, the Masser family left Eichelsdorf and came to America, entering the country through Ellis Island and making their way to Gettysburg. Elizabeth Masser was 22 years old and her parents John and Catherine Muth Masser were 60 years old and 56 years old, respectively. The family name has alternately been written as Moser in the family Bible or Maser in the family genealogy. It was rumored that Elizabeth Masser left a fiancée in Germany when her family moved to America.

Peter Thorn, Elizabeth's future husband, was the son of Philipp Thorn and Miss Van Diefenbach. He was born in Reckershausen (Prussia), resided in Fischbach and arrived in America two years before the Massers. He was 26 years old. Peter sailed on the ship Wheland from Bremen, Germany through London and arrived in the Port of New York on April 20, 1852. The first place he settled was Johnstown, Pennsylvania but the reason he came to America was to study copper mine feasibility in West Virginia. He was a mining engineer by trade. His exploits in West Virginia were short-lived. Within two years of arriving in the United States, he had made it to Gettysburg. In the fall of 1854, he was working for the *North American Mining Company* in its copper mine on High Street. The entrance was under the old convent, two doors west of St. Francis Xavier Church. The building is still standing today. The mine failed within a short time when the shaft filled with water.

Some time between their separate arrivals in Gettysburg and September 1, 1855, Elizabeth Masser and Peter Thorn met, courted and became engaged. As it turned out, September 1, 1855 was a significant day for Elizabeth and Peter in a couple of ways. First, it was their wedding day. Second, it was the day that the cornerstone was laid for what would be their residence for 19 years. On the day of their wedding, church bells all over town rang. Elizabeth, thinking the bells were rung to celebrate her marriage, asked her new husband how everyone knew. In reality, the churches all over town were ringing their bells to commemorate the cornerstone- laying ceremony for the new Gatehouse and Lodge of the town's Evergreen Cemetery. The Lodge was finished in November of that year .

Daguerreotype of Peter and Elizabeth Thorn around the time of their marriage. (Brian Kennell/Evergreen Cemetery)

In February of 1856, Peter Thorn was chosen as the "Keeper of the Cemetery," and Peter, Elizabeth and her parents all moved into the Gatehouse and began to settle into their lives as a new family.

In exchange of his caretaking responsibilities, Peter received an annual salary of $150.00 per year and he and his family could live in the new Gatehouse rent-free. In exchange for a place to live and an annual salary, Peter was expected to perform the following duties, as laid out in the *By-Laws and Regulations of the Cemetery*:

- *To reside upon the premises and not absent himself form the grounds without permission of the President*
- *Lock and unlock the gates daily*
- *Keep the avenues and walks in order*
- *Keep the grounds clean and the shrubbery and trees trimmed*
- *Attend to the visitors*
- *Deal with the trespassers*
- *Prevent chickens, pigs or cows to roam at large on the grounds*
- *Dig graves for all interments within the Cemetery*

In 1858, Peter purchased a plot of land near Pennsylvania College (now Gettysburg College) on North Washington Street and began to build a home. This home was to be a typical modest, but comfortable, lower-middle class home. They had planned to have Elizabeth's parents live with them in the home, which was not uncommon during that time period. Peter, Elizabeth and her parents never lived in this house. Rather, they remained in the Cemetery Lodge for 20 years.

The Thorns new occupation as resident caretakers of the Evergreen Cemetery is comparable to an average laborer's wages during the time period. A typical laborer would earn about $650.00 per year. But, a modest annual rent was between $500 and $600 per year. This left the wage earner with between $50.00 and $150.00 to spend on other needs. Elizabeth was able to supplement her husband's income by performing domestic chores for their neighbor, Captain John Myers. Captain Myers' home was right next to the Evergreen Cemetery and later became the Soldiers' Orphans Homestead.

Drawing of Evergreen Cemetery Gatehouse by Don
Reinhart; copyright Evergreen Cemetery 1998
(Brian Kennell/Evergreen Cemetery)

The Gatehouse was comprised of two separate sections. The south and north sides were mirror images of each other but there was no passageway that connected the two. The family had to step outside to get from one section of the "house" to the other. Each side had two floors above ground and a cellar. Elizabeth's parents, John and Catherine, lived in the south half while Peter and Elizabeth lived in the north half. The Cemetery business office was located on the ground floor of the south side and this cellar was used for storage. The ground floor on the north side was the parlor, the cellar was the kitchen and the newlywed's bedroom was located on the second floor.

Life progressed normally for this average mid-nineteenth century couple, which meant that the extended family fit comfortably within the four rooms of the new Gatehouse. But, soon the family began to expand as children started to arrive. In July of 1856, the first of their eight children was born. They named him Frederick and he served an early and pivotal role in keeping the family together.

Family lore states that sometime after the baby's arrival in 1856, the fiancée that Elizabeth had left behind in

Germany showed up on her doorstep at the Gatehouse. He pleaded with Elizabeth to leave with him. She was torn and unsure what to do until she heard baby Frederick crying and instantly knew she had to stay. Peter thanked Elizabeth for her decision by buying her a new dress.

In 1858, Elizabeth and Peter had another son and named him George David. In 1860 Peter decided that he no longer needed the house he had built for his new family on North Washington Street back in 1855 and he sold it to the widow Sarah Bath.

In February of 1861, a third son was born and named John. This young family now had four adults and three children under the age of four living in the four rooms of the Gatehouse. The two babies probably slept in their parent's room while the oldest, Frederick, most likely slept with his grandparents in their room.

Not long after John was born the Civil War erupted, dividing the nation. The Thorns lived another year within their daily routine, probably following the progress of the war in the local newspapers until the summer of 1862.

The House built by Peter Thorn in 1858 for his family, but they never lived at this location – they resided in the Evergreen Gatehouse for the first twenty years of their marriage. (Sue Boardman)

Captain John Myers' home just north of the Gatehouse where Elizabeth did domestic chores to supplement the family's income. In 1866, the building became the National Soldiers Orphans Homestead. (Boardman Collection)

Modern view of Elizabeth and Peter Thorn's bedroom, on the north side of the gatehouse looking out toward East Cemetery Hill. (Jennie Knox, Gettysburg Photo, LLC.)

Modern view of the entryway, cupboard and window bench in Catherine and John Masser's bedroom, on the south side of the gatehouse, looking into the cemetery grounds. (Jennie Knox, Gettysburg Photo, LLC.)

Section Three:
Surviving Civil War

On August 1, 1862, Peter, along with nearly a hundred and fifty other Adams County citizens, enlisted at Gettysburg for a term of three years. A recruiting office was set up in the clothing store of Gettysburg businessman, George Arnold, on the southwest corner of the town square on Chambersburg Street. At age 36, Peter mustered into the service three weeks later with Company B of the 138th Pennsylvania as a Corporal. He received a $25 bounty for his signature and would receive another $25 when his term of service was up. In October, he was promoted to 4th Corporal and on December 6 he was promoted to 3rd Corporal.

(See Peter's war service and company history in Section Twelve)

When Peter joined the army, Elizabeth assumed the role of the Cemetery Caretaker. In addition to her household duties, including taking care of her three small children and looking after her aging parents, she added the duties of the caretaker that were outlined in the previous chapter.

By late June 1863, Elizabeth had a new complication that made all of her previous homemaker duties and her yearly caretaker duties just a little bit harder. Elizabeth was six-months pregnant and life was only just beginning to get tough.

On Friday, June 26, 1863, the war that was raging in the South for two years finally made its way north toward Gettysburg. A portion of the Confederate army, under General Early, passed through Gettysburg on June 26 looking for supplies. General Early "made requisition on the town for supplies consisting of flour, potatoes, onions, pork, shoes, etc." While the town Council was busy dealing with the General and his requests, Elizabeth was busy dealing with six of his soldiers. She recounts:

"Six of them came up the Baltimore Pike. Before they came into the Cemetery they fired off their revolvers to scare the people. They chased the people out and the men ran and jumped over fences...I was a piece away from the house... When they rode into the Cemetery I was scared, as I was afraid they had fired after my mother. I fainted from fright, but finally reached the house...They said we should not be afraid of them, they were not going to hurt us like the yankeys [sic] did their ladies.

They rode around the house on the pavement to the window, and asked for bread and butter, and buttermilk... My mother went and got them all she had....and just then a rebel rode up the pike and had another horse beside his. The ones who were eating said to him: "Oh, you have another one." And the one who came up the pike said: "Yes, the ----- ----- shot at me, but he did not hit me, and I shot at him and blowed him down like nothing, and here I got his horse and he lays down the pike." (The man whom the rebel had killed was Sandoe, who had composed a company in Gettysburg.)

He turned around to me [and] asked me: "Is that a good horse over there?" It was our neighbor's horse, and I said: "No, it ain't. It is a healthy enough horse, but he is very slow in his motions." Well, it would not suit. I knew if the horse was gone the people could not do anything, so I helped them.

Soon they went to different places where they destroyed the telegraph and the railroads. Evening came on and they had destroyed a good many of the cars, and burned the bridge and seven cars on it. This was the Rock Creek Bridge. We could see the cars drop down from Cemetery Hill." Next morning we heard that there was a small battle at York. Everywhere they destroyed all they could. But, Elizabeth and her family were only just beginning to experience the fear and horror that would come with the impending battle.

The Evergreen Gatehouse from glass plate negative by Alexander Gardner, July 1863. (Library of Congress)

The Evergreen Gatehouse from glass plate negative by Mathew Brady, July 1863. (Library of Congress)

Detail of Gardner's Gatehouse image showing two young boys sitting on the stoop – probably Fred and George, the two oldest Thorn Boys. (Library of Congress)

Section Four:
Witnessing the Battle of Gettysburg

As July began on a Wednesday morning, the worst fear of the citizens of Gettysburg began to unfold. A battle had begun on the outskirts of town and would soon sweep through the streets.

While Peter Thorn was serving in Maryland Heights near Harpers Ferry with the 138th Pennsylvania Regiment, two great armies were concentrating at Gettysburg.

By the afternoon, they fell back through town and redeployed on Cemetery Hill.

From the upstairs windows of the Gatehouse, Elizabeth could see the battle as it was beginning across town to the northwest. Through the morning, as she was baking bread, she began to notice Union soldiers coming into the Cemetery by way of the Taneytown Road. Today, this would be the back way into the Cemetery. These Union soldiers set up a cannon position just across the road from the Gatehouse and in the Cemetery itself. She recalls:

"We were trying to feed them all we could. I had baked in the morning and had the bread in the oven. They were hungry and smelled the bread. I took a butcher knife and stood before the oven and cut this hot bread for them as fast as I could. When I had six loaves cut up I said I would have to keep one loaf for my family, but as they still begged for more I cut up every loaf for them.

We had all the glasses and tins and cups and tubs and everything outside filled with water. All the time our little boys were pumping and carrying water to fill the tubs. They handed water to the soldiers and worked and helped this way until their poor little hands were blistered.... and the vessels were kept filled with water for the thirsty soldiers, and were quickly emptied. They would take a drink and hurry off, and this lasted until the pump broke."

In the afternoon, as the battle action began to approach the south side of town, Elizabeth took her children and parents and went down to their cellar. However, it was not long until her curiosity got the better of her and she went back into the house to see how the battle was progressing. Soldiers were all around her property and she overheard one of them say that a guide was needed. The Union army was shooting its own men because they were unfamiliar with the countryside. Elizabeth recalled the discussion and how, "shortly afterwards a big man with straps on the shoulders came along and asked me whether there was a man about who could point out the roads."

She explained that her father was German and would not be understood, and her son was only 13 and too small. She offered to go along with him herself. He initially declined, citing the danger – it would have been unchivalrous of him to ask her to go. But, Elizabeth insisted. She felt that there was as much danger inside as outside the house. He finally accepted her offer.

Elizabeth and the officer set out. As they walked, the officer had Elizabeth stand on the right side of his horse to shield her. She guided the officer over the fields and roads, all the way to the York and Harrisburg Roads on the northeastern edge of town, which was several miles from the Gatehouse.

Elizabeth remembered the journey and the reaction of the Union soldiers to a woman being in their midst:

"We walked through flax, and then through a piece of oats, and then we stood in a wheat field. They all held

15

against me coming through the field, but as he said I was all right, and it did not matter, why they gave three cheers and the band played a little piece, then I walked a little past a tree to where I could see the two roads. I showed him the Harrisburg Road, the York Pike, and the Hunterstown Road. It was with one of General Howard's men that I went. Then he took me back home."

All the way home, this officer again ensured that Elizabeth walked on the safe side of the horse.

Upon their return to the Gatehouse, Elizabeth was again curious about how the Union boys were faring, so she began to climb her staircase to the bedroom upstairs to get a better look. As she climbed, she noticed that a shell had come through the window and lodged in the ceiling. She wisely returned to the cellar with her parents and children.

Near sundown, a soldier arrived at the Gatehouse and went down to the cellar to find Elizabeth. He asked her to make supper for General Howard, the 11th Corps Commander, who had made his headquarters on Cemetery Hill. She complained that she had no bread to offer since she had given it all out earlier that day. The messenger replied that she "could make cakes," and that they, "were good enough for war times."

Unconvinced that dough cakes would be sufficient for the General's supper, Elizabeth ventured over to her neighbor, Captain Myers', house where she was storing some of her meat for safekeeping. She went over just after dark intending to bring back some of the four hams and a shoulder that she had stored there. When she arrived at his house, she could not find any of the family members. What she did find were many wounded soldiers. She saw "...a lot of men lying in rows, and six of them did not move..." The scene upset her so much that she immediately left the house without bothering to retrieve the meat.

Elizabeth started preparing supper. Her family ate as they waited for General Howard. The supper table stood ready for a very long time. Finally, around midnight, Generals Howard, Slocum and Sickles finally arrived to have their meal. According to Elizabeth they ate, "...two good sized dough cakes...three pieces of meat I had...apple butter and coffee."

General Oliver O. Howard, Commander of the Union 11th Corps. Howard used the Evergreen Cemetery as his headquarters. (Library of Congress)

After they had eaten, Elizabeth asked General Howard whether the family should leave the house. He answered that they should stay put, go to the cellar when the fighting started at about daybreak, and he would send word if there was any danger; at which point they were to go right away and, "not study about it."

He also said that, if the family had any good things, he would see that they were taken to the cellar for safekeeping. Then he laughed and said, "I guess you think all your things are good." In fact, Elizabeth and her mother *had* brought some good linens from Germany so they placed them in a chest and had them carried to the cellar.

Later, the soldiers that carried the chest to the cellar made considerable noise in the process. Elizabeth said they should be quiet because, "General Howard had asked to lie down and might be asleep upstairs." The soldiers laughed at this and told her the General was busy out in the Cemetery, laying down tombstones to prevent their damage in the coming battle. The headstones may also have been laid down to protect the soldiers from shattered stone fragments.

The children may have slept that night, but Elizabeth and her parents did not and at 4 a.m. they went down to the cellar. They waited there for a couple of hours. In one account, Elizabeth mentions that there were 17 people total in the cellar including her family and some other civilians. In another account, she does not mention these "extra" people. In recalling that night, Elizabeth later remembered that, "the noise of the cannonading was terrible." At about daybreak, a man arrived and said, "This family is commanded by General Howard to leave this house as quickly as they can, to pick nothing up and take with them but their children." They were directed to travel away from town on the Baltimore Pike, keeping to the road where the soldiers could see them. The pace was slow because the road was filled with soldiers and wagons.

Elizabeth relates how a shell had exploded behind them: "When we were a little way down the pike a shell bursted [sic] back of us, and none of us were killed, but we commenced to walk faster." As they travelled down the road, they came upon a farm where the Sheafer family lived. She continued:

"We went down the pike one and one half miles when we began to feel weak and sick, we were so hungry, for we had eaten nothing the day before we were so scared when the battle commenced. The woman baked just like we did and we smelled the bread. She sold me a loaf for 25 cts....but the bread was doughy and we could not eat it."

Whether or not they were able to eat any of the fresh bread, Elizabeth and her family kept moving down the road until they came to the farm owned by George Musser. Elizabeth and her parents figured this farm was far enough out to be safe and they were tired of contending with all of the soldiers and wagons on the road. They stopped with the Mussers for the night.

Much like most homes in the area, the Musser's home was filled with soldiers. As Elizabeth looked into the rooms of the house, she "...saw rows of soldiers lying there, resting. One corner was vacant" and she thought that her "mother could lie there with the children." As the family was discussing the best course of action, Elizabeth recalled:

"About in the middle of one row a man raised himself on his elbow and motioned me to come to him. My father signed I should go to him, and he took a picture out of his pocket and on it was three little boys, and he said they were his, and they were just boys like mine, and would I please let him have my little boys sleep near him, and could he have the little one close to him and the others near him? And so, he took them and had them lying by him."

When Mrs. Masser and the boys settled in for the night, Elizabeth and her father decided to try to return to the Gatehouse to check on their hogs, their house and their belongings. Getting back was a challenge. The guards on the road were reluctant to let them through. Elizabeth and her father were finally allowed to pass once they explained that they lived in the Gatehouse and wished to return to retrieve some belongings.

As they arrived at the Cemetery and neared the barn they could hear the cries of the wounded men from the first day's fight. There were so many wounded and dead that they could not get near the house and had to find a man to help them get down to the cellar where they had stored their "good" things. To Elizabeth's horror and dismay, there were six wounded men in the cellar and her bedclothes were out and all around them. These, "poor wounded men were crying and going on so...they called to their wives and children to come and wet their tongues." The scene was so upsetting to Elizabeth and her father and their belongings were so strewn about that they were only able to grab a shawl before leaving the Gatehouse.

Mr. Masser went to check on the hogs and found that they disappeared, and so had their old stable, the pigpen and all of the wood. The soldiers had used every last scrap for fires.

Their mission thwarted, Elizabeth and her father returned to the Musser's house. No guards gave them any trouble on their journey back out of town. At about three o'clock in the morning, Elizabeth collected her mother and her boys and they set off further down the road headed toward White Church. When they arrived, they found many of their neighbors already there.

The Henry Beitler Place was nearby and being hungry and thirsty, Elizabeth set out to see what she could find. Mrs. McKnight joined her and together they decided to hunt through the house for something to eat, just like the men in the army. They found a barrel in the cellar. While Elizabeth held the lid, Mrs. McKnight thrust her arm in almost to the elbow and brought it out covered with soft soap. Elizabeth said, "That was the first laugh we had that day." They did eventually find two crocks of milk, which they used to soften the bread crusts they had brought with them. It was an unsatisfying meal that left them all still hungry.

There was a wagon shed at this farm where the wounded were brought and an amputation station had been set up. Elizabeth recalled, "…they brought the wounded and took off their limbs, and threw them into the corn crib, and when they had a two horse load they hauled them away."

Despite the sickening scene all around them, Elizabeth and her family were still hungry. She had to provide for her family and was unable to because of the army. She decided that since the army had benefitted from the food and supplies at her home, they could reciprocate, at least a little. She and Mrs. McKnight went to the front of the house and knocked on the door. When an officer answered, Elizabeth and Mrs. McKnight let him know that they wanted some food. The officer asked them if they knew Jennie Wade. Elizabeth replied that she knew her and that she lived near her home. He told her that Jennie Wade, as well as Maria Bennett from town, had been killed. Although Elizabeth later learned that Jennie had indeed died from a soldier's stray bullet, the report of Maria's death was inaccurate. The officer wrote out some orders, which the two women took to the provision wagon nestled in the woods a mile away. They returned with aprons full of coffee, sugar and hard-tack. Elizabeth saved some of the coffee and sugar as a keepsake and held onto them into her later years.

Henry Beitler and his family had sought refuge in Littlestown. Upon his return to the farm, he retrieved a barrel of flour he had nailed into one of his closets. He divided up the flour among the people staying on his place and Elizabeth spent the better part of the next couple of days baking bread, which the soldiers discovered and offered to pay her for it. She also spent time watching the wounded who were, "calling for water and screaming all the time." At one point, Elizabeth saw some of her furniture travelling down the road in her family's wagons. Her sons urged her to go out and stop them.

On Tuesday, July 7th Elizabeth and her family returned home to the Gatehouse.

This clock was taken from the family parlor by members of General Howard's staff and hung on the brick archway during the battle. It was found still keeping time when the family returned to the gatehouse.
(Brian Kennell/Evergreen Cemetery)

Section Five:
Living with the Battle's Aftermath

Elizabeth continued her story:

"On the way home, we met Mr. McConaughy. He was the president of the Cemetery at that time and he said to me, "Hurry on home, there is more work for you than you are able to do." So we hurried on home....There were no window glass in the whole house. Some of the frames were knocked out and the pump was broken. Fifteen soldiers were buried beside the pump shed. I went to the cellar to look for the food things I put there on the first night. One chest was packed with good German linen, others packed with other good things – everything was gone but three featherbeds and they were full of blood and mud. After I had dragged them out of the cellar I asked an officer...if I would ever get any pay for the things spoiled like this. He asked me what it was and I told him bed clothes that were in the cellar....he said in a very short way, "No!""

David McConaughy, wartime president of the Evergreen Cemetery Association. McConaughy met Elizabeth as she was returning to the Gatehouse after the Battle of Gettysburg and told her to "hurry on home, there is more work for you than you are able to do." (Brian Kennell/Evergreen Cemetery)

24

All of the furniture and all of their possessions were gone, not to mention their livestock and fences. The family beds that were used during amputations were ruined. "The legs of six soldiers had been amputated on the beds and had to be thrown away," she related. There were not even any clothes left for the family. Once their pump was fixed, it took Elizabeth, and several other women, four days to thoroughly clean the bloodied and muddied bedclothes that were left behind.

Ruined bedding and dirty bedclothes were not the only things that the army left behind. In one adjacent field lay fifteen dead horses, in another there were nineteen. None of these were buried or burned, and caused a terrible stench. Elizabeth said she could barely eat for days due to the disagreeable odor. The Thorn family lived in a tent, erected by the Hospital Corps, for a while because their house was uninhabitable.

Very shortly after her return home, she received a note from the president of the Cemetery. "Mrs. Thorn, it is made out that we will bury the soldiers in our Cemetery for a while, so you go for that piece of ground and commence sticking off lots and graves as fast as you can make them." Elizabeth and her father began marking off graves and digging them as fast as they could. John Maser, Elizabeth's father, was 65 years old. Elizabeth was six-months pregnant and wearing the clothes she had fled in, which by her account, included "a heavier dress than usual." She lived in that dress for six weeks!

The air in Gettysburg was filled with the stench of death and, to make matters worse, it was the middle of summer. Elizabeth and her father dug graves by themselves for two days and then finally enlisted some help. They sent telegraphs to friends to come and help, but only two came. Elizabeth paid their train fare to and from Gettysburg as well as a hefty daily wage. One friend stayed two days and the other stayed five before he became deathly ill and had to return home. Elizabeth and her father continued to dig. By the time the second friend departed, they had dug forty graves. In three weeks time they had dug 91 graves. The ground where the graves were placed was some of the rockiest in the cemetery. Elizabeth was never paid any additional wage for all of her extra work, from the Cemetery or from any other source. Her family received only the monthly caretakers' salary of $13.

In addition to the tremendous amount of work created for Elizabeth as a result of the battle, she continued to do all of the regular duties of the Cemetery caretaker. In September, young James Culp died when a shell he was attempting to open exploded. Elizabeth buried him, as well as other townspeople as necessary.

The Thorn family's damage claims filed with the War Department in the years after the battle showed that they suffered the loss of nearly all of their household furnishings, clothing, food, crops, and livestock. The total came to $395.00. They received $41.50 in payment, 20 years later.

When the Soldiers' National Cemetery was ready, 50 of the 91 bodies buried in Evergreen were exhumed and reinterred in their new plots. The families of the remaining men buried in the Evergreen Cemetery did not wish for their soldiers to be moved.

On November 1, 1863, three months after the last body was buried, Elizabeth Thorn gave birth to her fourth child, Rosa Meade, named after the Union commander at Gettysburg, General George Meade. Rosa was Elizabeth's first daughter. Sadly, she was not a very strong child and died at the age of fourteen. Elizabeth was also sickly for years following the battle.

There are no accounts of Peter Thorn arriving in Gettysburg to assist his wife with these grisly tasks. His unit, the 138th Pennsylvania, was stationed in Harpers Ferry during the first days of July. Elizabeth never mentions that he returned to help, but his company records list Peter Thorn as being on the descriptive list of deserters for the month of July 1863, returning to his regiment on the fourth of August. It was not uncommon for the soldiers in the Civil War to receive plaintive letters from home, telling them of the hardships their families were enduring and to please come home and help. Mostly, it was Confederate soldiers who were the recipients of such letters since most of the battles of the war were fought on their land. But it's not outside the realm of possibility that Peter Thorn received such a letter from his wife, given the gravity and magnitude of the situation.

On November 19th, 1863, just eighteen days after Rosa Meade was born, Elizabeth and her family saw the large crowds that assembled on Cemetery Hill to witness the dedication of the Soldiers' National Cemetery. President Abraham Lincoln gave his now famous Gettysburg Address in a poignant ceremony on Cemetery Hill. Modern photo-historians have determined that the platform upon which President Lincoln and the many dignitaries sat that day was physically located within the boundaries of Evergreen. The throngs of people in attendance stretched from Evergreen Cemetery all the way to the Taneytown Road and beyond.

Crowds gathered for the dedication of the Soldier's National Cemetery, November 19, 1863. Elizabeth and her sons were in the crowd to hear President Abraham Lincoln deliver the Engraving of Evergreen Cemetery on the November 19, 1863 dedication of the National Cemetery. Frank Leslie's Illustrated, December 5, 1863. (Boardman Collection) (Library of Congress)

Rocky ground in the area of Evergreen where Elizabeth worked to bury Union soldiers for several weeks after the battle. From a Weaver stereoview. (Boardman Collection)

Another view of the rocky ground in Evergreen Cemetery where Elizabeth buried Union soldiers. (Unknown photographer, Boardman Collection)

Gravestone for Fred Huber, a Union soldier from Gettysburg killed May 31, 1862 in the Battle of Fair Oaks. The stone was struck by artillery during the Battle of Gettysburg. (Brian Kennell/Evergreen Cemetery)

Grave stone for Esaias Jesse Culp which was damaged by artillery during the Battle of Gettysburg. Culp died in 1861 at the age of 53. (Sue Boardman)

The graves of nearly a hundred soldiers buried by Elizabeth in the weeks following the battle. (Sue Boardman)

East Cemetery Hill looking toward town shortly after the battle. Photographed by Timothy O'Sullivan, July 1863. (Library of Congress)

General view of the cemetery looking toward the Gatehouse. Elizabeth was responsible for the daily operations in addition to the extra work created by the battle. (Boardman Collection)

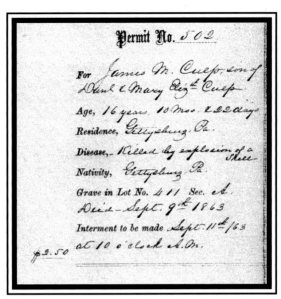

Burial permit for James Culp, 16, who died attempting to open a live shell he found on the battlefield. (Adams County Historical Society)

1st Lt. Herman Donath, aged 19, was from Roxbury, MA. He enlisted on 8/13/1861 in K Co., 19th MA Infantry. Lt. Donath was killed on 7/3/1863 at Gettysburg during the fight known as Pickett's Charge. (Sue Boardman)

Pvt. Aaron A. Clark, of Haddam CT, enlisted on 8/14/1862 into Co. G, 14th CT Infantry. He was killed on 7/3/1863 at Gettysburg and buried by Elizabeth Thorn in Evergreen Cemetery. (Sue Boardman)

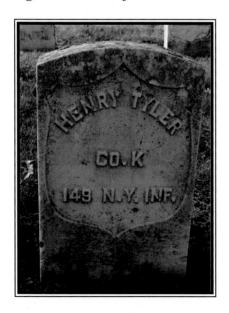

Pvt. Henry Tyler, age 21, enlisted at Baldwinsville, NY on 9/1/1862 into Co. K, 149th NY Infantry. He was killed on July 3 during the fight on Culp's Hill. (Sue Boardman)

Section Six:
Moving on After the War

The Battle of Gettysburg was not the end of the war. In fact, it lasted for two more years. During that time, Elizabeth continued to care for Evergreen Cemetery and her family while her husband continued to serve in his unit. Peter fell ill and was admitted to U.S. General Hospital in Alexandria, Virginia in March and April of 1864, complaining of rheumatism. He remained a patient there until July. On September 19, he was wounded at the Battle of Opequan in Winchester, Virginia and sent to a hospital in Philadelphia. Peter Thorn suffered a wound from a shell fragment three inches above his wrist joint on his left arm. He recovered almost fully from this wound. The 138th Pennsylvania witnessed Lee's surrender at Appomattox Court House and then continued on to serve in Richmond and Washington for a few more months before being mustered out of service on June 23, 1865.

Peter Thorn returned home to his wife, four children and his in-laws. He resumed his pre-war occupation as the caretaker of Evergreen Cemetery, and Elizabeth continued to assist him. There were now four children and four adults living in the Gatehouse. In 1866 Elizabeth had another daughter, Louisa Katherina, known as Lulu. That year Peter requested a raise from the Cemetery Board and they granted it. His annual income increased from $150 to $200 per year. A new addition was added to the north side of the gatehouse, but it was designated for the comfort and convenience of the pastor and not for use by the family. The crowded living conditions and possibly the difficulty of them using the ladder to the upper floor prompted Peter to move his elderly in-laws to a place in town, which he purchased for their use. They were now both nearly 70 years old.

In the summer of 1868, little Lulu died but another child, Harry Peter, was born. When Elizabeth's father, John Maser, died in 1869, Catherine Maser was brought back into the household to live and Peter sold the house in town. The following year, he bought eight acres of ground adjoining the Cemetery property to the south, a short distance down the Baltimore Pike. (Today The Pike Restaurant, formerly Big Bopper's Lounge, sits on the site.) Here, in 1871, Peter built a farmhouse. That same year the couple had another daughter, Lillie. Although Cemetery regulations required that the superintendent reside at the Gatehouse, in all probability, Peter received permission to live off the Cemetery premises since his property adjoined it. The family is shown in court records as paying taxes on the farm acreage, house and livestock kept there for the remainder of Peter's tenure as Cemetery Gatekeeper.

In 1873, Peter and Elizabeth had their final child, little Ehre Philipp, who only lived thirteen days. Elizabeth was now forty-one years old. Her household included her mother, Catherine; her husband Peter; and their six children raging in ages from two to sixteen.

By 1874, Peter Thorn was given a promotion to the post of, "Police Officer in Regard to Cemeteries." In 1875, he resigned as Gatekeeper of Evergreen having served nearly 20 years.

During the Thorns' tenure at Evergreen, a number of well-known citizens were buried there including Johnston "Jack" Skelly, Jennie Wade, Samuel Weaver, John Burns and Rev. Samuel S. Schmucker.

For the next three years, the Thorns enjoyed their much-earned peaceful existence on their little farm while Peter served as Superintendent of the Soldiers' National Cemetery. This period of tranquility was only marred by the death of then fourteen year-old Rosa Meade, who was weak and sickly most of her life.

By the late 1870s Gettysburg was a growing tourist destination, especially for Civil War veterans, and the hotel industry was booming. Peter became a part of this new development when he became the Proprietor of the Wagon Hotel, later called the Battlefield Hotel. Many of the classier hotels that catered to the veterans and other dignitaries were located around the town square. The Battlefield Hotel was situated at the intersection of two busy roads, the Baltimore Pike and the Emmitsburg Road, on the south end of town. Because travelers would encounter the Battlefield Hotel soon after arriving into the town from the South, this hotel saw its share of veterans and dignitaries too.

Although the children may have continued to stay at the farm with their grandmother, Peter's duties as proprietor required his presence at the hotel most of the time. Elizabeth undoubtedly shared the burden of keeping the fifty or so rooms clean and preparing food for the guests. Peter held a tavern license continuously from 1878 to 1884, which meant food and drink were served at the hotel.

The veterans liked to patronize establishments run by other veterans and the Battlefield Hotel was no exception. The hotel is mentioned in this article entitled, "PA Veterans Return to Gettysburg" printed in a Veteran's newspaper of 1882:

"A rendezvous place for the Grand Army boys is the Battlefield Hotel, about 100 yards from the camp and on the outskirts of town...at the junction of the Emmitsburg Rd. and Baltimore Pike. It was the outer post of the Union SS during the battle and bears visible evidence of the prominent position. The landlord, Peter Thorn, is himself a Grand Army Man, having served with the 138th PA throughout their campaigns." (The camp referred to above was usually held on East Cemetery Hill.)

After six years as tavern keepers, the Thorns at last retired to their farm for the long term, living there from 1885 until they sold it in 1901. During this time, Elizabeth's mother Catherine Masser died at the age of 92.

Elizabeth had spent all but three of her then fifty-eight years living in the same household as her mother. This means Peter had spent all but three of his thirty-five years of married life living with and looking after his mother-in-law.

In 1901, Peter and Elizabeth sold their farm and moved into town to a house they rented at 50 West Middle Street. This was their last move. They lived in this house for six years where, in 1905, Peter and Elizabeth celebrated their golden wedding anniversary. On January 8, 1907, Peter Thorn died at age eighty after suffering from complications of asthma. Elizabeth died ten months later on October 17. She had been sick for ten days and was staying with her daughter, Lillie (Mrs. Harry F. Young,) in Harrisburg at the time of her death. She was seventy-five. The Thorns were buried side-by-side in Evergreen Cemetery, a fitting final resting place for the people whose lives were so inextricably connected to it.

Elizabeth Thorn lived in Gettysburg throughout her entire adult life, in five locations, never living more than two miles from the town square. But it is for her experiences at the Cemetery and Gatehouse that she is most remembered.

Near the end of her life, in 1905, Elizabeth gave an interview for the *Gettysburg Compiler*, in which she recounted her experiences during the Battle. With the recording of her story, Elizabeth joined the ranks of a number of local women who endured hardships during the Battle of Gettysburg and overcame the challenges for which they would be remembered. But, the added burdens placed upon Elizabeth Thorn make her deserving of a special place among these heroines of Gettysburg.

Grave of Jack Skelly, mortally wounded in June 1863. He was reportedly engaged to Virginia Wade, the only civilian killed during the Battle of Gettysburg. (Brian Kennell/ Evergreen Cemetery)

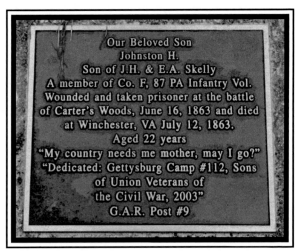

Plaque describing the inscription of the Skelly marker which became difficult to read over the years. (Sue Boardman)

The original grave marker for Virginia (Jennie) Wade. (Brian Kennell/Evergreen Cemetery)

The modern grave marker on Jennie Wade's grave in Evergreen Cemetery. (Sue Boardman)

The original grave of John Burns, the Gettysburg civilian who joined the battle on July 1. He was buried in Evergreen in 1872, during the time the Thorns were caretakers. (Brian Kennell/Evergreen Cemetery)

The original stones over the graves of John Burns and his wife Barbara were destroyed by vandals. In 1904, this new stone was placed by the members of Gettysburg's G.A.R. Post.

The Reverend Samuel S. Schmucker, founder of the Lutheran Theological Seminary and Pennsylvania College, died in 1873 and was buried in Evergreen by the Thorns. (Brian Kennell/Evergreen Cemetery)

The grave of James Gettys, founder of Gettysburg. Gettys died in 1815 and was moved to Evergreen in 1865 from his original burial site. Tyson stereoview, 1867. (Boardman Collection)

The grave of Samuel Weaver who died in 1871 after being run over by a train. Weaver superintended the exhumations of Union soldiers for reburial in the National Cemetery. (Sue Boardman)

Tipton and Co. stereoview of the new addition to the Evergreen Gatehouse, circa 1868. Captioned "Residence at Ever Green Cemetery" (Boardman Collection)

The Wagon Hotel. Peter Thorn served as proprietor from 1878 to 1884. The hotel and tavern were located at the intersection of Baltimore Street and Emmitsburg Road. Tipton and Co. stereoview. (Boardman Collection)

The Wagon Hotel. Tyson stereoview, circa 1867. (Boardman Collection)

Pennsylvania Grand Army of the Republic encampment on East Cemetery Hill, July 1880. Many of the veterans stayed at the Wagon Hotel. (Boardman Collection)

General view by W.H. Tipton of the Soldier's National Cemetery. Peter served as Superintendent of the National Cemetery for three years after he resigned as caretaker of Evergreen. (Boardman Collection)

The house at 50 West Middle Street where the Thorns spent the remaining years of their life. (Sue Boardman)

Section Seven:
The Evergreen Cemetery and Gatehouse

The first part of this book has been dedicated to the first caretakers of the Evergreen Cemetery: Peter Thorn, and his family. This chapter will be dedicated to the Evergreen Cemetery and the Gatehouse itself.

The Evergreen Cemetery was founded in 1854 and opened in November of that year. Gettysburg had grown to the point where the townspeople needed a public cemetery where all, regardless of creed, could be laid to rest. Previous to this date, the citizens were buried in the small cemeteries associated with and attached to the various local churches.

The first burial, which was of Mrs. Daniel Beitler, was officiated by the Reverend Jacob Zeigler.

When the Evergreen Cemetery opened, the rates for grave digging were: $1.50 for children under six, $2 for children ages six to fifteen, and $2.50 for adults.

On June 2, 1855 the "Gate Way and Lodge" were authorized by the Cemetery Association. George Henry Chritzmann was the lowest bidder, giving the association a price of $1,025.00 for the work. The cornerstone was laid on September 1, 1855 and the church bells all over town tolled in honor of this event. On February 8, 1856, the association chose Peter Thorn as the first Keeper of the Cemetery. He and his family were allowed to live in the Gateway Lodge, rent-free. Additionally, he was paid an annual salary of $150.00. Also in 1856, the ladies of the town held a fair to benefit the installation of a walk in the Cemetery and the association purchased a kitchen stove for the Lodge.

On July 13, 1863, the President of the Evergreen Cemetery Association (David McConaughy) was authorized to sell, "fractions of lots" for burial of the soldiers. These lots were sold for between $2.50 and $2.80. The President was also charged with purchasing lands adjoining the Evergreen Cemetery for the purpose of soldier burial. The officers of the association were tasked with contacting military authorities for the removal of those soldiers who were, "irregularly buried" during the fight on the grounds of the Gateway Lodge.

A month later, the association charged Mr. McConaughy with selling these newly acquired lands to the Commonwealth of Pennsylvania, at the proposal of Mr. David Wills, Esq., for the cost price. These lands would be used for the burial of dead soldiers. In this same resolution is the wording that provides for, "an open iron railing enclosure of ordinary height" to be made and maintained by Pennsylvania on the line between these new lands (now turned over to Pennsylvania) and the Evergreen Cemetery.

In its first 100 years, the Evergreen Cemetery had only five Keepers, each one serving for many years. As the years progressed from the Battle, the local churches requested, and were granted, permission to relocate the dead in their cemeteries to this hallowed location. The fact that the Evergreen Cemetery played such a crucial role in the Battle and that it adjoined the Soldiers' National Cemetery made it a desirable location as a receptacle of the dead from other, smaller, cemeteries. There was also a plot designated for the children who died at the Soldiers Orphans' Home in town and a plot for deceased students from Pennsylvania College.

In 1885, an addition was added to the north side of the Gatehouse.

With all these extra burials, the Evergreen Cemetery added land as the years passed. In 1913, a 12-acre tract was added that was divided from the main part of the Cemetery by a Right-of-Way on which the Gettysburg Electric Railroad operated their trolley from the downtown area out to Little Round Top. Eventually, the Gettysburg Electric Railroad went out of business and the U.S. Government acquired all of the Right-of-Ways on which the trolley operated.

Because this strip of land bisected the Evergreen Cemetery, the association wanted to regain ownership. In 1945, they approached the Department of the Interior and presented their case. The answer they received was a proposal for a land exchange. The Department of the Interior had their eye on several patches of land around the battlefield, but they did not have the money to acquire them. They proposed that the Cemetery Association purchase one of these plots of land and exchange it for the old Right-of-Way plot that bisected the Cemetery. On September 22, 1948, the exchange was made. The Cemetery Association had purchased five acres of land on the west side of West Confederate Avenue, a piece of the McMillan land, and exchanged the deed of this new parcel for the deed to the parcel that ran through the Cemetery.

In 1965, a maintenance garage was built on the northwest side of the Gatehouse. A Veterans' area was opened in Section U in 1979. Instead of the traditional government slab stones, Two-part gravestones provided longevity and aesthetic beauty to the memorial space.

Restoration work on the Gatehouse was performed in 1999, which included repointing of the brickwork. The following year, the flagpoles at the graves of John Burns and Jennie Wade were replaced. In 2009, the process began to place avenue signs at intersections throughout the Cemetery to reflect names known to exist in the late 19th century.

Their stewards have lovingly cared for the Gatehouse and Cemetery landscape since 1854. Their history and appearance will continue to enthrall visitors to the hallowed ground of Gettysburg thanks to these dedicated caretakers:

Evergreen Cemetery Caretakers
Peter Thorn 1856 – 1875
William Pfeffer 1875 – 1895
Harry S. Trostle 1895-1920
Sandoe Kitzmiller 1920 – 1947
Howard Kitzmiller 1947 – 1974
Glenn Chronister 1974 – 1976
Arthur Kennell 1976 – 1991
Brian Kennell 1991 – Present

Scenic walkway in Evergreen. Tipton and Co. stereoview. (Boardman Collection)

Image of Evergreen Cemetery and Gatehouse from stereoview by Charles J. Tyson, 1867. (Boardman Collection)

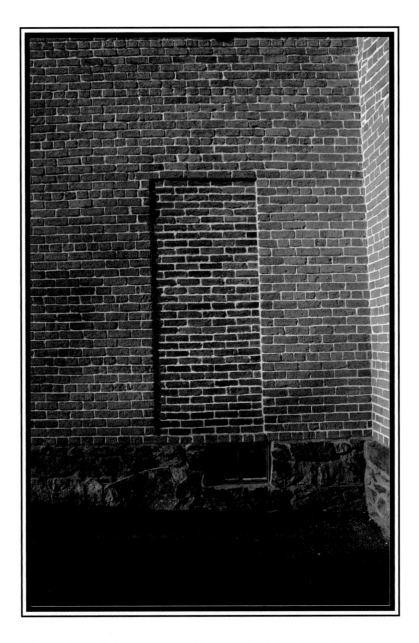

The original doorway in the north side of the Evergreen Gatehouse which was filled in many years ago. There is an identical doorway in the south side. There was never a direct connection between the two sides.

Section Eight
Ron Tunison and the Gettysburg Civil War Women's Memorial

In the early 1900s, Elizabeth left a couple of accounts of her experience during the Battle of Gettysburg. But since then, unless someone purposefully set out to learn about the people who lived in the Gatehouse during the battle, visitors would not generally run across Elizabeth Thorn and her family. The same is true for so many of the women of Gettysburg who were left to clean up the mess of battle.

In 2002, the Evergreen Cemetery Association addressed this omission by erecting a memorial to the women civilians who served during and after the battle. The Gettysburg Civil War Women's Memorial was placed 50 feet southwest of the Gatehouse during a ceremony 148 years after the founding of Evergreen Cemetery. The memorial is a bronze statue depicting Elizabeth Thorn, six-months pregnant, and in the midst of her grave digging duties. The statue of Elizabeth "will serve to forever commemorate the meritorious deeds of the countless women who served in various capacities during the Battle of Gettysburg." (Dr. Walter Powell at dedication of statue, November 16, 2002).

There was a long road to travel to reach the memorial's dedication date. After deciding in 2000 to erect the memorial, the Cemetery board's first step was to select a sculptor. After speaking with the Superintendent of Gettysburg National Military Park, local art dealers, retailers and historians, the choice was clear. The Evergreen Cemetery Association selected Ron Tunison of Cairo, New York for the commission. Tunison had the best reputation around for historical integrity and the quality of his work was widely displayed on Civil War battlefields. Previous to this commission, Tunison had three sculptures already on the Gettysburg battlefield: *General Samuel Crawford Monument* on Little Round Top, the *Friend to Friend Masonic Memorial* in the Soldiers' National Cemetery, and the *Delaware State Monument* adjacent to the old Cyclorama parking area near the Maryland monument.

His excellent reputation wasn't confined to just Gettysburg. In 2000, the Capital District Civil War Round Table awarded Tunison recognition as "Civil War Artist of the Year" for his artistic ability and for his work to raise money for battlefield preservation. "Ron is the most respected monument-maker in the country today," said the Round Table's spokesperson, Sue Knost.

The next step in the process was to research the subject. Tunison is especially meticulous in researching his historical statues. He consults with historians in a number of disciplines to get even the smallest details correct. For example, Tunison consulted Juanita Leisch, author of *Who Wore What?: Women's Wear, 1861-1865* to assist him in correctly depicting Elizabeth Thorn's dress and bonnet. In a newspaper article printed in the *Albany Times Union*, (December 10, 2000,) the artist described the importance of research. "Accuracy is what I hold most important," Tunison said, "The equipment, the buttons, the hats…it all has to be exact."

When the research was completed, it was time to begin creating the model. There were project sketches and clay models of different versions until just the right pose and expression were achieved. After all of the elements aligned, it was time to make a maquette (a sculptural scale model or rough draft). The research, drafts and maquette were the most time-consuming tasks to complete.

Once the maquette was approved, Tunison began work on the full-sized rendering. He worked in his studio, located in a 19th century barn, to sculpt the full-sized Elizabeth Thorn in clay. To help him take the maquette to full-sized, he used a panagrah, which is a machine that traces the lines of the example and translates them into those same lines in a larger scale to make a copy. The full-sized model was created in pieces, since the final 7-foot bronze casting needed to be done in several pieces as well.

Upon completion of the full-sized model, a mold was made to shape the bronze for the final steps in the process. Tunison used the lost-wax process during which the mold is always completely destroyed.

With the mold completed, it was time to pour the bronze, which was done at a special foundry. When the individual pieces were poured and set, they were assembled and joined together. The joints were sanded and polished and a special patina was added with a combination of heat and acid. The finished sculpture was packaged and shipped to Gettysburg.

The statue arrived in early November and was placed on a specially prepared spot near the Gatehouse. On November 16, 2002 it was dedicated during a ceremony presided over by local dignitaries and authors. The then-current president of the Cemetery Association, Dr. John F. Schwartz, had the honor of unveiling the statue along with the artist. Descendents of Elizabeth Thorn were on hand to lay a wreath at her feet. While the day was gray and rainy, there was an excitement in the air. Finally, Elizabeth Thorn would be visible to all of Gettysburg's visitors. It would now be harder to overlook the invaluable contributions she and her fellow townswomen made to the soldiers who fought and died there.

One of the several preliminary drawings by Ron Tunison for the Elizabeth Thorn statue in Evergreen Cemetery, 1997. (Brian Kennell/Evergreen Cemetery)

Another preliminary drawing by Ron Tunison. (Brian Kennell/Evergreen Cemetery)

Original drawing which won the award of the monument contract for Ron Tunison. (Brian Kennel/Evergreen Cemetery)

Two-foot high model or maquette based on the sketch. (Alice Tunison)

Sculptor Ron Tunison putting the finishing touches on the two-foot maquette. (Alice Tunison)

Unveiling the miniature sculpture, November 29, 2000. Brian Kennell, Superintendant of Evergreen Cemetery, Sculptor Ron Tunison, Arthur Kennell, retired Superintendent of Evergreen Cemetery. (Sue Boardman)

A seven-foot maquette being produced from the two-foot one. A framework or armature is built and then the clay is added over it. (Alice Tunison)

A panagrah is used to reproduce the larger model from the small one while keeping the dimensions correct. (Alice Tunison)

Sculptor Ron Tunison using artifacts and research to achieve historical accuracy. (Alice Tunison)

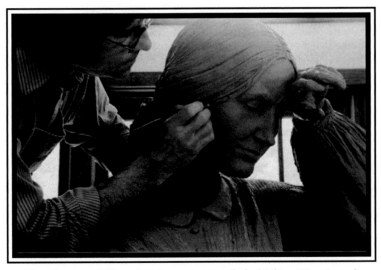

Tunison adding texture to model. (Alice Tunison)

The seven-foot maquette, from which the actual bronze statue is made, is produced in two sections. (Alice Tunison)

The completed seven-foot maquette. From this, a mold will be made (destroying the maquette) which will then be used to make the finished bronze piece. (Alice Tunison)

Sculptor Ron Tunison next to the newly-dedicated statue in Evergreen Cemetery, November 16, 2002. (Dave Getty)

Gettysburg Civil War Women's Memorial in Evergreen Cemetery. (Dave Getty)

Section Nine:

Elizabeth and Peter Thorn in Gettysburg, 1855 to 1907

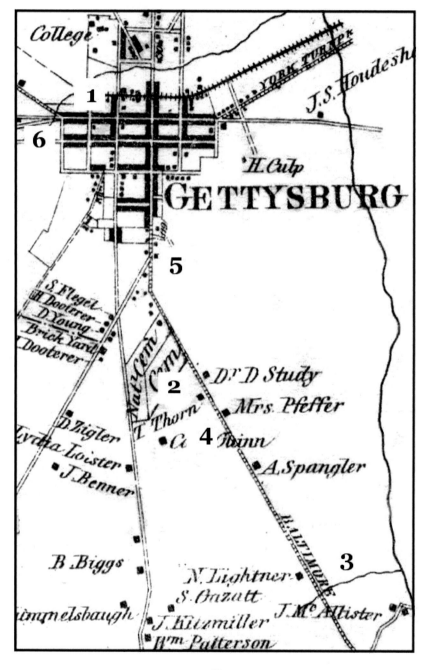

Peter and Elizabeth Thorn lived in five different locations in Gettysburg during their 52-year marriage; all five within a two-mile radius of the town square.

1. 225 North Washington Street: 1856 to 1858 - Peter built a house here for his new bride but the couple never lived in the home.

2. Evergreen Cemetery: 1856 to 1875 -The Thorns lived at this location in the gatehouse and served as caretakers for the cemetery.

3. Elizabeth took her family to a farm house further south down the Baltimore Pike on the morning of July 2 and remained there until July 5.

4. The Thorns built a farm house on the Baltimore Pike in 1871 and resided there from 1876-77, and again from 1885 to 1901.

5. The Thorns lived at the Battlefield Hotel at the intersection of Baltimore Street and Steinwehr Avenue from 1878 to 1884 when Peter was the proprietor of this establishment.

6. 50 Middle Street: 1902 to 1907 – Peter and Elizabeth lived in this rental home during the last five years of their lives.

Section Ten:
The Thorn Family Tree

Elizabeth Moser Thorn Born in Eigelsdorf, Germany December 28, 1832; died October 17, 1907 in Gettysburg, PA. Aged 74, buried in Evergreen Cemetery. Married Peter Thorn September 1, 1855.

Daughter of **John Masser** (1797-1869) and **Catherine Muth Masser** (abt. 1799-1890). Both parents died in Gettysburg and are buried in Evergreen Cemetery.

(John) Peter Thorn Born in Reckershausen, Germany January 24, 1826; died January 8, 1907 in Gettysburg, PA. Aged 80; buried in Evergreen Cemetery.

Children of Peter and Elizabeth (all born in Gettysburg):

Frederick Born July 15, 1856; died 1917. Married Sarenda Sterner (1859-1920). Both are buried in Evergreen Cemetery. Fred worked as a barber in Gettysburg for many years.

George David Born August 19, 1858; died March 8,1937. Married Charlotte E. Mickley (1858-1895). Both are buried in Evergreen Cemetery. George worked as a clerk for the State of Pennsylvania in Harrisburg.

John Born February 6, 1861; died 1932. Married Mia M. Comfort (1863-1942). Both are buried in Evergreen Cemetery. John worked as a carpenter and also ran a livery in Gettysburg.

Rosa Meade Born November 1, 1863; died August 28, 1878 Age 14 years; buried in Evergreen Cemetery.

Louisa Katherina (Lulu) Born July 8, 1866; died December 24, 1868. Age 2 ½ years; buried in Evergreen Cemetery.

Harry Peter Born July 1, 1868; died December 17, 1961. Age 93; buried Rosedale Cemetery, Martinsburg, WV. Married Mary Elizabeth Livers (1872-1956).

Lillian Elizabeth (Lillie) Born February 1, 1871; died December 22, 1954. Age 83; died in Hagerstown, MD. Married (Harry) Frank Young (September 25, 1865; died August 2, 1946). Both were born in Gettysburg and are buried in Evergreen Cemetery. The family was living in Harrisburg in 1907 where Lillie's mother Elizabeth was staying when she died.

Ehre Philipp Born May 8, 1873; died May 21, 1873. Age 13 days; buried in Evergreen Cemetery.

Image of Elizabeth Thorn taken a few years after the war. (Brian Kennell/Evergreen Cemetery)

Peter Thorn wearing his Grand Army of the Republic (GAR) membership badge. Peter hosted the returning veterans at the Wagon Hotel and participated in their activities as one of them. (Cynthia Thorn Baynham)

Image of Elizabeth Thorn in middle age, by unknown photographer. (Brian Kennell/Evergreen Cemetery)

Image of Peter Thorn in middle age, by unknown photographer. (Brian Kennell/Evergreen Cemetery)

Painting of Elizabeth Thorn by an unknown artist. (Brian Kennell/Evergreen Cemetery)

Painting of Peter Thorn by an unknown artist.
(BrianKennell/Evergreen Cemetery)

Catherine Masser, Elizabeth's Mother.
(Cynthia Thorn Baynham)

Section Eleven:
Thorn Family Obituaries

Elizabeth Thorn
Star and Sentinel, October 23, 1907

Mrs. Elizabeth Thorn, widow of the late Peter Thorn, died at home of her daughter, Mrs. Harry Young, in Harrisburg, Thursday morning about 7 o'clock from pleurisy aged 74 years, 9 months and 19 days.

Mrs. Thorn has not been in the best of health for some time on account of her advanced years, but she was able to go about. She had been to Martinsburg, W. Va., to see her son, Peter, and while returning home contracted a severe cold from an open car window, resulting in pleurisy.

Mrs. Thorn was one of Gettysburg's most highly esteemed women. She was known by nearly every resident of this place where she spent her entire life.

Throughout her long and useful career she was a prominent figure in this historic town. During the battle of Gettysburg, Mr. Thorn was at Maryland Heights, serving his country in the capacity of a soldier, while his noble wife, the subject of this sketch was at the gateway house of the Evergreen Cemetery baking bread, caring for the Union soldiers and superintending affairs at the cemetery.

Mrs. Thorn was the most kind-hearted Christian woman; she was ever ready to help those in distress or affliction. She possessed an extraordinary sunshiney disposition and her life was typically and nobly happy. The realization that she possessed many warm friends gave her a merry heart.

Mrs. Thorn's maiden name was Elizabeth Moser. She was married Sept. 1, 1855, and during that year they moved to the Evergreen Cemetery where they resided for 20 years. Mr. Thorn departed this life on January 8th last.

Deceased is survived by the following children: George D., Chief Clerk of the State Department, Harrisburg; Frederick and John, of this place; H. Peter, of Martinsburg, W. Va., and Mrs. Harry Young, of Harrisburg.

The funeral was held Saturday afternoon at 2 o'clock, from the residence of her son, George D. Thorn, West Middle Street, Rev. J. A. Clutz, her pastor, officiated. Interment in Evergreen Cemetery. The floral tributes were many and most beautiful, indicating the esteem in which deceased was held.

Rosa Meade Thorn
Gettysburg Compiler, August 29, 1878

Died, on Friday last, in this place, Rosa Meade, oldest daughter of Peter and Elizabeth Thorn, aged 14 years, 9 months and 22 days. The funeral on Sunday afternoon was largely attended. St. James Lutheran Sunday School, of which the deceased was a member, turned out in a body, and sang at the grave one of her favorite songs.

Peter Thorn
Gettysburg Compiler, January 16, 1907

Peter Thorn, who spent more than fifty years of the eighty years of his life in this place passed away at his home on West Middle Street on Tuesday evening January 8th, aged 80 years, 5 months and 15 days. He had been ill for several weeks with asthma, though a sufferer from that disease for several years. Peter Thorn was known to everyone, young and old, and for everyone he had a genial warm hearted greeting, which attracted and made it a pleasure always to meet and talk with him. He was ever held in high esteem. He was born on the banks of the Rhine and came to this country when a young man. In 1854 he located in Gettysburg and soon made himself known for his many good qualities. September 1, 1855 was the date fixed for his marriage to Miss Elizabeth Masser and on that day all the church bells of the town were rung and when the bride inquired of the groom the cause of the ringing, she was informed that the Evergreen Cemetery had been dedicated that day. Neither of the two dreamed that the coincidence of that day was to be marked by further association for more than 20 years. When a superintendent was chosen for the new cemetery the choice fell upon Peter Thorn and he made a most efficient officer. He resigned in 1874. Peter Thorn was a veteran of the Civil War, enlisting in Co. B, 138th Regt. In 1862 for three years and was promoted to a corporal and served until honorably discharged in 1865. He participated in battles Brandy Station, Locust Grove, Wilderness, Spotsylvania, Cold Harbor, Petersburg, Monocacy, Winchester, Fisher's Hill, Cedar Creek, Capture of Petersburg and Appomattox. His wife with her parents resided at the Cemetery Gatehouse during the battle here. The funeral was held on Friday afternoon, Rev. Dr. J. A. Clutz conducting the services and a burial squad of the Sons of Veterans under Capt. Wm. McG. Tawney doing the last rights of a burial with honors of war. He leaves his wife, four sons and one daughter, George Thorn, Fred Thorn, and John Thorn of this place, Peter Thorn of Martinsburg, W. Va. and Mrs. Harry Young of Harrisburg.

The grave of Rosa Meade Thorn who died in 1878 at the age of 14. (Sue Boardman)

The graves of Peter and Elizabeth Thorn in Evergreen Cemetery. (Gettysburg Daily)

Section Twelve:
Peter Thorn's Regiment:
The 138th Pennsylvania Volunteer Infantry

By the summer of 1862, it became apparent that the Civil War was not going to end as quickly as everyone had hoped. President Lincoln made a call for 300,000 troops and every state and county had to send their quota. An advertisement in Gettysburg's *Star and Banner* newspaper on July 17th, 1862 read "ADAMS COUNTY TO ARMS!" The "patriotic, able-bodied men of Adams County" answered the call, signing up for three years of service. They would be designated as Company B and G, 138th Pennsylvania Volunteers. Company B was raised in the town of Gettysburg and was initially led by Captain John F. McCreary. McCreary was a student at Pennsylvania College (now Gettysburg College) when the war broke out and organized students into a militia unit and drilled them in preparation to defend their community.

A recruiting office was set up in the clothing store of Gettysburg businessman George Arnold, located on the southwest corner of the town square on Chambersburg Street.

By August 12, Captain McCreary had enlisted about one hundred men in Gettysburg. They travelled to Harrisburg by rail and reported for duty at Camp Curtin the following day where the 138th Pennsylvania Volunteer Infantry was formed. Uniforms and equipment were distributed and military instruction began.

Peter Thorn, gatekeeper of the Evergreen Cemetery, became a corporal of the company that included many of his friends and acquaintances.

Here is a brief history of the regiment recorded in *The Union Army, Volume One*:

One Hundred and Thirty-eighth Infantry. - Cols. Charles L. K Sumwalt, M. R. McClennan; Lieut.-Cols. M. R. McClennan, Lewis A. May; Majs., Lewis A. May, Simon Dickerhoof. The 138th was composed of men from the counties of Montgomery, Adams, Bedford and Bucks, and was mustered into the U. S. service at Camp Curtin, Harrisburg during the latter part of August and the first part of Sept., 1862, for a term of three years.

On Aug. 30, 1862, before the regimental organization was completed, it moved to Baltimore and was there employed in guarding the Baltimore & Ohio railroad, with headquarters at the Relay house until the middle of June, 1863, when it moved to Harper's Ferry where it was assigned to Elliott's brigade of French's division. On the evacuation of Harper's Ferry on July 1, it moved to Washington, thence to Frederick, Md., and joined in the pursuit of Lee as part of the 3d corps.

It was under fire but not active at Wapping Heights and during the remainder of the fall shared in the various marches and counter-marches during the Virginia campaign, being engaged at Brandy Station with small loss, and in the Mine Run campaign at Locust Grove, where it behaved with great gallantry and repulsed repeated charges, losing 7 killed, 45 wounded and 3 missing, Col. McClennan being among the wounded.

It then went into winter quarters at Brandy Station, Col. McClennan resuming command on March 13, 1864, and on May 3 it moved on the spring campaign, attached to Seymour's Brigade, Rickett's (3d division, 6th corps. It suffered severely at the Wilderness, losing 27, killed, 94 wounded and 35 missing. It shared in the fighting at Spotsylvania, but its losses there were small, as it was not heavily engaged. At Cold Harbor it shared in the gallant assaults of the division losing 7 killed, 54 wounded and 7 missing.

Crossing the James, it went into the trenches at Bermuda Hundred; later joined its corps before Petersburg; shared in the movement on the Weldon railroad at Reams, station; and moved with its division in July to Monocacy, where it was hotly engaged against the forces under Early on the 9th, its losses in the battle being 68 killed, wounded and missing.

After re-joining its corps, it shared in the various maneuvers between Washington and the Shenandoah Valley. Gen. Sheridan now assumed command of the Army of the Shenandoah, composed of the 6th, 8th and 19th corps. The 138th formed part of the cavalry support at Smithfield; was actively engaged at the Opequan and Fisher's hill, losing in the two engagements 46 killed, wounded and missing, shared in the pursuit of the enemy to Harrisonburg; returned with the army and encamped at Cedar Creek, where it was warmly engaged in the battle in October, losing 42 killed and wounded.

In the early part of November the regiment was encamped at Philadelphia and then returned to Winchester. In December, it moved with its corps to Petersburg and was detailed as garrison for Fort Dushane. While stationed there it received a Christmas present of a beautiful stand of colors from the "loyal citizens of Norristown and Bridgeport, Pa." On April 1, 1865, it rejoined the corps and on the 2nd shared in the final assault on the enemy's works at Petersburg. It then joined in the pursuit of Lee's army, taking a large number of prisoners. It was active at Sailor's creek, where it fought its last battle. After the surrender of Lee, it made a forced march with its corps to Danville, Va., but was not needed by Gen. Sherman, so it returned to Richmond and proceeded thence to the vicinity of Washington, where it was finally mustered out of service on June 23, 1865.

The total enrollment of the regiment was 955. It had 51 killed in action, 339 wounded, 31 missing. Killed and died of wounds during service 94, died by disease and accident 54, captured 48.

Service:
Duty at Relay House, Md., till June, 1863.
Moved to Harper's Ferry, W. Va., June 16.
Escort stores to Washington July 1-5.
Join Division at Frederick, Md., July 7.
Pursuit of Lee July 7-24.
Wapping Heights July 23.
Bristoe Campaign October 9-22.
Advance to line of the Rappahannock November 7-8.
Kelly's Ford November 7.
Brandy Station November 8.
Mine Run Campaign November 26-December 2.
Payne's Farm November 27.
Demonstration on the Rapidan February 6-7, 1864.
Dirty at and near Brandy Station till May.
Rapidan Campaign May 4-June 12.
Battles of the Wilderness May 5-7; Spotsylvania May 8-12; Spotsylvania Court House May 12-21.
Assault on the Salient May 12.
North Anna River May 23-26.
On line of the Pamunkey May 26-28.
Totopotomoy May 28-31. Cold Harbor June 1-12.
Before Petersburg June 17-18.
Jerusalem Plank Road, Weldon Railroad, June 22-23.
Siege of Petersburg till July 6.
Moved to Baltimore, Md., July 6-8.
Battle of Monocacy July 9.
Pursuit of Early to Snicker's Gap July 14-24.
Sheridan's Shenandoah Valley Campaign August to December.
Charlestown August 21-22.
Battle of Opequan, Winchester, September 19.

Fisher's Hill, September 22.
Battle of Cedar Creek October 19.
Duty at Kernstown till December.
Moved to Washington, D.C., thence to Petersburg, Va., December.
Siege of Petersburg December, 1864, to April, 1865.
Fort Fisher, Petersburg, March 25, 1865.
Appomattox Campaign March 28-April 9.
Assault on and fall of Petersburg April 2.
Sailor's Creek April 6.
Appomattox Court House April 9.
Surrender of Lee and his army.
March to Danville April 23-27, and duty there till May 23.
March to Richmond, Va., thence to Washington, D. C., May 23-June 3, Corps review June 8.
Mustered out June 23, 1865.

Losses:
Regiment lost during service:
6 Officers and 90 Enlisted men killed and mortally wounded and 1 Officer and 70 Enlisted men by disease.
Total 167.

Dyer, Frederick H., *A Compendium of the War of the Rebellion*, 1908

Bibliography:

"Everyday Life During the Civil War", Michael J. Varhola; Writer's Digest Books, Cincinnati, OH; 1999.

"The Light of the Home: An Intimate View of the Lives of Women in Victorian America", Harvey Green; Pantheon Books, NY; 1983.

"Women at Gettysburg", Eileen F. Conklin; Thomas Publications, Gettysburg, PA: 1993.

"Early Photography at Gettysburg"' William A. Frassanito; Thomas Publications, Gettysburg, PA; 1995.

"Beyond the Gatehouse: Gettysburg's Evergreen Cemetery", Brian A. Kennell, The Sheridan Press, Hanover, PA; 2000.

"Atlas of Adams County, Pennsylvania", *I. W. Field & Co., Philadelphia, PA; 1872.*

"The Young Lady's Book", William Hosmer; Derby & Miller, Auburn; 1851.

"History of Ever Green Cemetery...with By-Laws & Regulations", Star & Sentinel Printing, Gettysburg, PA; 1905.

Adams County Historical Society:
      Thorn Family File
      Excerpts from Elizabeth Thorn's diary
      Excerpts from Minutes of the Evergreen Cemetery
Association
      Gettysburg Tax Records 1855-1907
      Cumberland Township Tax Records 1855-1907
      Gettysburg Compiler obituaries, published Tavern
      Licenses, and advertisements

Census records
Architectural Review Board files re
historical buildings in Gettysburg
Gettysburg and Adams County map collection
Gettysburg Street Directories, 1800, 1888, 1896, 1903
Naturalization Papers

Interviews:
<u>Brian A. Kennell</u>, Superintendent and Historian, Evergreen Cemetery.
<u>Elwood W. Christ</u>, Asst. Director, Adams County Historical Society and Member Historical Architectural Review Board of Gettysburg.
<u>Cynthia Thorn Baynham</u>, Thorn descendant, Martinsburg, WV.

National Archives Record Group 92, Quartermaster Claims; National Archives, Wash. DC

Boardman Photograph Collection

About the Authors:

Kathryn Porch is a Foreign Service Officer with the United States Department of State. Born and raised in Florida, Kathryn's love for the Gettysburg battlefield led her to Gettysburg College where she graduated with a B.A. in English in 2002. She worked several jobs just out of college but found her way back to Gettysburg as Operations Coordinator for the Gettysburg Foundation, where she was instrumental in the completion of the Museum and Visitor Center. In 2009, Kathryn joined the Department of State and to date has served diplomatic tours in Ghana and Kyrgyzstan.

Sue Boardman, a Gettysburg Licensed Battlefield Guide since 2000, is a two-time recipient of the Superintendent's Award for Excellence in Guiding. Beginning in 2004, Sue served as historical consultant for the Gettysburg Foundation for the new museum project as well as for the massive project to conserve and restore the Gettysburg cyclorama. She has authored a book on the history of the Cyclorama entitled **"The Gettysburg Cyclorama: A History and Guide."**

Sue currently serves as the Leadership Program Director for the Gettysburg Foundation. Her program, *In the Footsteps of Leaders* has been well-received by corporate, non-profit and educational groups.

Sue is a native of Danville, PA and an Honors Graduate from Penn State/Geisinger Medical Center School of Nursing. A 23 year career as an ER nurse preceded her career at Gettysburg. Sue served as President of the historic Evergreen Cemetery Association as well as adjunct instructor for Harrisburg Area Community College and Susquehanna University. Her articles have been published in several Civil War journals.